My Sheep

By Heather Miller

Welcome Books

SCHOLASTIC INC.

New York Toronto London Auckland Sydney
Mexico City New Delhi Hong Kong Buenos Aires

Photo Credits: cover, pp. 5, 7, 9, 11, 13, 15, 17, 21 by Thaddeus Harden; p. 19 © Index Stock Imagery

Contributing Editor: Jennifer Ceaser
Book Design: MaryJane Wojciechowski

ISBN 0-516-23884-1

12 11 10 9 8 7 6 5 4 3   5 6 7/0

Printed in the U.S.A.   10

First Scholastic printing, March 2002

Contents

My name is Audrey.

Welcome to my sheep farm!

4

This is Belle.

Belle is a **ewe**.

A ewe is a mother sheep.

7

This is Belle's **lamb**.

A lamb is a baby sheep.

9

A lamb can always find its mother.

The lamb just has to listen for her special **bleat**.

A bleat sounds like this: "Baaaaaaa!"

I feed my sheep **grain**.

They eat the grain from a **trough**.

My sheep grow coats in the winter.

Their coats are called **fleece**.

Fleece keeps the sheep warm when it is cold.

15

In the spring, Dad shaves off the fleece.

It doesn't hurt the sheep.

It's like giving the sheep a haircut!

The fleece is made of **wool**.

The wool is used to make **yarn**.

19

At night, my sheep go to sleep in a **pen**.

The straw on the floor keeps them warm.

Goodnight, my sheep!

21

New Words

bleat (bleet) the sound a sheep makes

ewe (yu) a mother sheep

fleece (flees) a sheep's coat

grain (grayn) food that sheep eat

lamb (lam) a baby sheep

pen (pen) a place where sheep are kept

trough (trof) something that holds food for farm animals

wool (wul) what a sheep's coat is made of

yarn (yarn) thick thread made from wool

To Find Out More

Web Sites

Barnyard Buddies
http://www.execpc.com/~byb/
Meet the Barnyard Buddies and learn more about farm animals.
Play animal games and send an e-mail to your favorite animal!

Sounds of the World's Animals—Sheep
http://www.georgetown.edu/cball/animals/sheep.html
Click on a sheep's picture and listen to it bleat!